Character Building in Youth

ALSO BY DOROTHY R. SWYGERT

A. G. Gaston: Make Your Dream Come True
Healing the Nation
The Oak Leaf
The March for Justice
The Mustard Seed Collection
Black Trilogy Plus

Character Building in Youth
THE POETRY WORKSHOP

I Am Somebody

Dorothy R. Swygert

REKINDLE THE HEART, HAMPTON, VIRGINIA 2010

Character Building:
THE POETRY WORKSHOP
I Am Somebody

Copyright © 2010 Rekindle the Heart

All rights reserved. No part of this book may be reproduced, stored in a retrieval system, or transmitted by any means, electronic, mechanical, photocopying, recording, or otherwise, without written permission.

Printed in the United States of America
Library of Congress Card Number: 2010902955
ISBN: 978-0-9648737-7-3

Cover Design by Norman Hocker and James R. Ward

Rekindle the Heart
P. O. Box 219
Hampton, VA 23669

Dedicated to the conditional high school seniors who used this model in my group counseling sessions to realize their goal of high school graduation and to students around the globe who are striving to develop their gifts and talents to make this a better world

Table of Contents

Introduction 1
Believe In Yourself 2
Self-Awareness 4
Don't Procrastinate 6
The Solitary March 8
The Tie That Binds 10
Satan Got A Hold On The Children 12
Who's Training The Children? 14
Passing The Torch: Family Reunion 16
Today 18
A State Of Being 20
Love And Time 22
Mix-Match 24
Selective 26
The Happy People 28
The Complex Man 30
Happiness 32
The Nuclear Teen 34
The Littlest Babe 36
The Loafer Shoe 38
The Oephoebic Oath 42
A Pledge Of A Full-Fledged Human Being 44
From Your Daughter, Dad, On Father's Day 46
Mothers Are Special 48
Family Heritage On Father's Day 50
Define The Role Of A Father In Our Times 51
Spread Your Wings 52
Dare To Be Different 54

Addendum
Personal Growth And Development 57

My Career Preparation 58
Setting Goals And Reaching High 59
My Biography (Brainstorming) 60
My Philosophy Of Life 61
Worthy Home Membership: Family Devotion 62
Volunteer Services: Resume Builder 63
Individual Assessment: My Gifts And Talents 64
A Community Analysis 65
Building Community Today For Tomorrow 66
Courtesy & Reconciliation 67
I Am Somebody: Cultivating My Life With Hope 68
Take Away Package 70
About Dr. Dorothy R. Swygert 93
Dr. Swygert's Lantern To Parents And Guardians 94

Introduction:
The Poetry Workshop
Character Building

Writing is a beautiful gift to foster in young people as they move through the developmental stages of life. Whether the person is writing a poem, a story, a play or just a journal, a rich outlet for self-expression is born. This book is a resource to involve young people in the thinking process through writing. As they begin to grasp deeper meaning they gain more knowledge and become more aware of their inner being resources. One basic goal of this writing workshop is to inspire the minds of youth and to motivate them to become more in tune with their inner self.

What can a young person learn by perceiving the inner being? A storehouse of knowledge lies within each individual. When an individual taps into this great reservoir, a new phase in an individual's life will unfold. As this opening takes place, one's life just may take on new meaning.

What are some things one may find in this human bank? At first, the individual may become more familiar with self and the developing personality surrounding self. After further and more frequent self-exploration, the individual may come to identify dormant skills, talents and gifts that are pleading to come alive. These self-discoveries may help the individual to answer the frequently asked personality question, "Who am I?" One will learn to respond to other questions and make a comparative analysis, like who am I compared to another individual or compared to a group?

Writing has an intrinsic value. The more one engages in the writing process, the more an individual is likely to probe into the inner being and learn more about one's selfhood. Knowing self can become very rewarding. An individual can learn about likes and dislikes, learn how to make intelligent choices and good decisions, assess gifts and talents and begin to make strides towards establishing a philosophy of life. One will soon develop the confidence to answer many questions readily and with composure. What do I like about myself? What is my purpose in life? What are some things I need to change in my life? What are my strengths and what are my weaknesses? What are some things I can do to help maximize my strengths and to reduce my weaknesses? How can I use my gifts and talents to contribute to making this a better world? This poetry book is offered to youth as a character building workshop. I offer this book as a challenge to young readers to seek, to explore, and to develop their inner being to realize their greatness. Enjoy the journey!

Dorothy R. Swygert

Dorothy R. Swygert

Believe in Yourself

When you believe that you can
And others believe that you can't
Just believe in yourself and do the best you can do
In striving to unfold the future for you.

Your task in life, your purpose to fulfill,
Your dreams to be accomplished
With a determined will.
Believe in yourself!

Believe in Yourself

1. What should you do if others say you cannot achieve a goal?
2. Is it important to believe in yourself? Why or why not?
3. If you do less than the rest, should you believe in yourself?
4. Do all people have the same talents and abilities? Explain.
5. People who believe in themselves should strive hard to:
6. The title *"Believe in Yourself"* explains a person's main purpose or task in life. What is the main task?
7. How does the poet suggest that people can accomplish their dreams in life?
8. Why is it important to believe in yourself?
9. What did you like best about this poem?
10. What would you add to this poem?

Dorothy R. Swygert

Self-Awareness

Self-awareness, what are you?
An inner feeling that helps one to be true,
To know, to explore, and to recognize all of your being,
To develop your talents that lie within!

Self-Awareness

1. What is self-awareness?
2. How do you define an "inner feeling?"
3. How does the "inner feeling" give direction in your life?
4. Is it important for one to be in touch with all of his or her being?
5. How does a person engage in exploring his or her whole being?
6. When a person explores his or her whole being, what are some things he or she may find or discover about him or herself?
7. Is it healthy to be true to yourself? Why or why not?
8. What did you like most about the poem "Self Awareness"?
9. What would you add to the poem?
10. What did you like least about the poem, "Self-Awareness"?

Dorothy R. Swygert

Don't Procrastinate

You're always talking about what you're going to do,
Yet you never set goals to make them come true.
You may want to do all of this in your heart,
But certainly you must get up and play your part

For dreams don't materialize unless you take a stand.
You have to organize yourself and write a plan
On what you want to do and the necessary steps to take
To make your dreams come true.

For life moves swiftly and life moves fast,
If you're not careful, you'll find that it has passed,
So get up and don't procrastinate,
Use your energy to open the talent gate!

Don't Procrastinate

1. What are goals?
2. What should people do if they would like to accomplish their goals?
3. Is it enough to want to do things in your heart? What else must the person do?
4. What does the writer mean in line 5?
5. Is time important in life? Explain.
6. What is the mood of the writer? How does she feel about procrastinators?
7. Is there a tone of urgency in the writer's message? What line shows this urgency?
8. What is the "talent gate"?
9. How should people use their energy?
10. What message does the writer leave in the mind of the reader?

Dorothy R. Swygert

The Solitary March

Let the drummer march to the beat of his own music,
Then let the human being be guided by the rhythm that one plays
So, in tune, one will walk in concert to one's own ways:

One's knowledge to develop,
One's path to hew,
One's future to carve out
To one's self to be true.

It does not matter if one has to stand alone
For there's a celestial guidance with a peaceful tone,
Although lonely, sometimes, one may be,
Just remember there is a Holy One, watching over thee.

The Solitary March

1. How does the poet compare this poem to life?
2. What does the poet mean in line 1 of the poem?
3. Why is it important for a person to, "walk in concert to one's own ways"?
4. How can being in tune with one's self help a person in life?
5. What should a person always be to him or herself?
6. When people march to the beat of their own music, what do people usually come to face? Do they have a lot of friends all the time? Explain.
7. What kind of road does a person travel on "The Solitary March"?
8. What is the basic goal of the person who travels on "The Solitary March"?
9. What did you like most about this poem?
10. What would you add or change?

Dorothy R. Swygert

The Tie That Binds

The tie that once bound
the community
together
has been broken.

Now there is a loose
gathering of
the home, church,
school, and community.

The tie that once bound them together
had a grip of
LOVE.

The home nurturing the newly born,
The church in quest of right
With its guiding light,
The school with its training rules,
And the community recycling and reinforcing
The values, morals and standards of
The home, church and school
Working, harmoniously, to produce
Posterity for a brighter tomorrow!

Character Building in Youth: The Poetry Workshop

The Tie That Binds

1. What is a tie? What is the purpose of a tie? Describe the meaning of "tie" in this poem.
2. What is the mood of the poet? Is the poet happy, sad or mournful?
3. What was the purpose of the tie in this poem? What role did it once play in the neighborhood?
4. A synonym is a word that has the same or a similar meaning as another word. What synonym could you substitute for "tie" in this poem?
5. What role did the home play in the child-rearing process?
6. According to the poet, what role did the church play in the child-rearing process?
7. How did the members of the community participate in the child-rearing process?
8. How did the school contribute to the child-rearing process?
9. Write a definition for "posterity."
10. The poet writes, "the home, church and school working harmoniously to produce posterity for a brighter tomorrow." Explain the meaning of this statement.

Dorothy R. Swygert

Satan Got a Hold on the Children
Dorothy R. Swygert

Satan, Satan, why are you so strong?
You're tempting millions of children to do wrong,
Innocent children sent from the hands of God,
You're doing everything in your might to make them depart
From their Christian values and their Christian heart,
You're luring them away to join the wicked chord.

Metallic music, they listen to by night and day
And direct their thoughts to evil along the way,
Sex, drugs and violence are constantly on display
And making them vulnerable to secular prey.

Yes, yes, yes I know, you say they can make their choice
But you have an upper hand, with your luring voice,
You tell them how they can gain the wealth of the world
Where you twist and warp their minds into a whirl,
Riches of the world you may, wickedly, give,
But eternal life, they will never be able to live!

Satan Got a Hold on the Children

1. The poet has portrayed Satan as a symbol of strength. Why has the poet described him as being a strong figure? What line in this poem supports your response?
2. What form of competition does the poet present in this poem? What are the two forces?
3. What has the poet identified as weapons used by Satan to lure people to him?
4. A "prey" is something to be taken and consumed as worldly food. Give the meaning of "secular prey" in this poem.
5. According to the poet, what methods does Satan use to "tempt" people? How does temptation influence the decision-making process?
6. Temptation is a choice between good and evil. Why is evil able to consume millions of people each day? Identify the line that supports your response.
7. What role does music play in your life? What is your favorite music? How long does this music remain in your mind?
8. The oldest battle in nature is said to exist between good and evil. Do you support this statement? Why or why not?
9. Why does the poet describe Satan as having "an upper hand"?
10. According to the poet, what is the benefit of making the best choice?
11. Bonus: Describe a situation when you were confronted with making a choice between good and evil, between right and wrong.

Dorothy R. Swygert

Who's Training the Children?

Well now, what did happen to our generation of today?
They have not been trained and they go astray,
Innocent they are, trying to find their own way
But without Biblical guidance, they're vulnerable to Satan's prey!

Character Building in Youth: The Poetry Workshop

Who's Training the Children?

1. What does it mean to be "innocent"?
2. Why is the poet concerned about today's generation?
3. Imagine you have received permission to write a line in this poem, how would you describe the children of today's generation? What are they doing? How are they living?
4. Is there a good relationship between the parents and children? Why or why not? Support your response.
5. An inferred meaning allows the reader to identify clues and symbols to arrive at a definition. Use the inferred clues in this poem to answer the questions below: According to the poet, the children of today's generation have not been trained. What is the poet's implied message? Are the children without parents and guardians? Explain why these statements have been made.
6. Has the poet placed the sole responsibility for training upon the parents and guardians? If not, list other people and agents who should take part in training children?
7. Explain the meaning of the phrase, "They're vulnerable to Satan's prey." Are there things that can be done to prepare children to resist temptation by making good choices and intelligent decisions?
8. What is the decision-making process? What factors should one consider before making a decision?
9. What is Biblical guidance? Where can one learn Biblical guidance? Name three examples of principles related to Biblical guidance.
10. Identify one experience in your life where you made the wrong decision. What were the consequences? What did you learn from this experience? What can you share with others to prevent them from making a similar error?

Dorothy R. Swygert

Passing the Torch: Family Reunion

It is a beautiful act when families come together in love
Putting aside their busy schedules to honor the
family seed which sprang from above,

Grandmas, grandpas, uncles, aunts, cousins, friends and kin
All come together to set a family trend.
The babies, the toddlers and teenagers will all play their part,
They will remember their relatives long after they DEPART
And that's what a family reunion is –

The gathering of the TREE as it sprouts through the years,
Each branch grows and models its own shape
And every little one must develop its own traits,
With tears, joys and laughter spent in a little while
We gather our family packs to return across the miles
But the most important theme is for the family
To keep the watch
That every generation must remember to pass the
FAMILY TORCH!

Passing the Torch

1. What event is taking place in this poem? Support your answer by describing those in attendance.
2. What is the bond in this gathering?
3. What symbol or metaphor does the poet use to describe the people in attendance?
4. Explain the line, "Each branch grows and models its own shape." What does the branch symbolize?
5. What is the purpose for this gathering? Identify one line in this poem to support your response.
6. Is this a local gathering? If not, share the line which supports your answer.
7. In a general contest, the torch is defined as "a light to be carried in the hand". Explain the poet's definition of torch as described in this poem.
8. A generation may be defined as "the average period of time between one succession of children and the next following (about twenty-five years)". What responsibility has the poet defined for each generation?
9. Draw a tree and place on it the groups of relatives who usually attend a family reunion.
10. Bonus Assignment: Do you have younger siblings? Are you a positive role model/mentor for them? Give two examples.

Dorothy R. Swygert

Today

Can you recall the past without being lost in yesterday?
Go forth beyond the yesteryears without
losing your way?
For yesterday is spent, past and gone
And today is before you, where you tread life's
marathon.

The past is alright to view
If you are able to admit that
your perceptions to you are true
in all that you do!

If you cannot view the past with an open mind that's true
to you
Then, steer your thoughts straight forward into today
Until you're able to objectively find
Strength to prod your way.

Character Building in Youth: The Poetry Workshop

Today

1. Write a definition for yesterday, today, and tomorrow.
   a) Yesterday:
   b) Today:
   c) Tomorrow:
2. What does the poet mean in line four, *And today is before you, where you tread life's marathon?*
3. According to the poet, what are perceptions?
4. What does it mean to be described as having an open mind? Give an example.
5. Is it a wise thing to do to look at the past? Why or why not?
6. The reader is asked to live in what period of time?
7. Should a person review the past if he or she has an inadequate perception of time?
8. According to the poet, what has happened to yesterday?
9. What do you like most about this poem?
10. What would you add or change about *Today?*

Dorothy R. Swygert

A State of Being

My depression got the best of me today,
All of my yesterday, today, and tomorrow collided
into one,
My dreams did not appear to be so real,
My ambition seem to just stand still
And as I tried to rise above
I felt a heavy force holding me back
Diminishing my strength to engage in creativity and
Preventing me from stepping in tune with time
To do all that could be done in one day
And leaving me, vulnerable, to secular prey!

A State Of Being

1. What is depression?
2. Describe the attitude of the person in this poem.
3. What happens to a person who is sometimes faced with depression?
4. What happens to dreams when a person is overcome with depression?
5. How does a state of depression affect a person's ambitions?
6. What happens to a person's creativity and time when one is in a state of depression?
7. Describe line ten, "And leaving me, vulnerable, to secular prey!"
8. According to the poet, is the person in this poem trying to overcome depression?
9. Have you ever been in a state of depression? If so, what would you suggest as ways to deal with this state of being?
10. What would you change about this poem?
11. Bonus: Webster's dictionary defines depression as a state of being sad. Write three sentences describing situations that can cause a person to enter into a state of depression.

Dorothy R. Swygert

Love and Time

Love bursts anew in many shades and colors,
There is no special place to fall in love,
Its setting is not crucial in the development,

What is most important is the magnetic nexus
Of the two, so tightly woven together,
Can one tell the exact moment when love has securely
Knitted its course?

No! The human eye cannot perceive the time of the solace bond
When it began, how it developed, or the course that
It will run!

Love and Time

1. What is the main idea in this poem?
2. Do you share this belief with the poet? If so, why or why not?
3. Does the poet believe there is a special time to fall in love? Explain
4. What is your definition of love?
5. What influence can love have in a person's life?
6. How can one tell when love is taking shape in one's life?
7. Explain the adage, "You may fall in love, but you will just have to be patient and give it time." Do you agree or disagree with this statement?
8. You have heard some people say, "What do you see in that person for you to be so in love"? Explain this statement.
9. In your opinion, "Can one tell the exact moment when love has securely knitted its course"? Explain.
10. Write a brief poem about "Love and Time". You may create your own title.

Dorothy R. Swygert

Mix-Match

He likes the beer joints and the lowly hotel bars,
I like the quiet side of nature without the scars,
He is restless in a cultural setting
And I am uncomfortable in his with constant fretting,
His heart is kind and his effort is great
But there is something that prevents us from being mates,
He loves the street life with all the laughter and
free life,
I like the quiet setting without the strife,
So when we are together, we are mix and match,
I guess I'll just have to wait for another catch!

Mix-Match

1. What is the poet describing in the poem Mix-Match?
2. Do these two people have similar life styles and the same interests?
3. Webster's dictionary defines mood as "a conscious state of mind or predominant emotions." What is the mood in this poem? Is it a mood of happiness or sadness? Explain.
4. Can the mood be changed in this poem? If so, how? If not, why not?
5. What does it mean to have something in common with a person or a mate?
6. In your opinion, what is the poet's meaning? What does it mean to have "free life" in this poem?
7. Describe what it means to be uncomfortable? Name three things that make you uncomfortable in a social setting.
8. What is a cultural setting? Give an example.
9. Identify one quality the person in this poem likes about her mate.
10. What is meant by "the quiet side of nature?"

Dorothy R. Swygert

Selective

I love a man with a creative mind
With a heart that is warm, sincere, and kind,
I love a man who is true and real,
Inquisitive of life, beyond a thrill
With a mind perched on a purpose and a plan
On how he can live his fullest life span.

I love a man who is not satisfied with mere mediocrity
But is willing to explore all his abilities.

I love a man with scintillating conversation
That enlightens my mind with mental stimulation.

I love a man who is strong and kind,
One of honest character and
Peace of mind.

Selective

1. What does it means to be "selective"?
2. If you were seeking a mate for the poet, what three characteristics would you place on your list?
3. What does it mean to have a "purpose for living"?
4. Is the poet seeking a well-rounded person? Explain. Refer to the lines that supports your response.
5. Write a definition of mediocrity. Should one feel satisfied with living a life of mediocrity? Why or why not?
6. Webster's dictionary defines integrity as being "the quality of wholeness and honesty; behavior in accordance with a code of values and morals." What line in the poem expresses integrity for you?
7. What does it mean to explore all of your abilities?
8. Explain the phrase, "enlightens my mind with mental stimulation".
9. What does it mean to be "strong and kind"? Can someone be strong as well as kind? Is strength usually associated with meanness and kindness is usually associated with weakness? Explain your answer.
10. Write three sentences describing a person "of honest character".

Dorothy R. Swygert

The Happy People

I like the happy people with a lot of smiles and laughter,
Bright, twinkling eyes and heartfelt grins
Expressing all the joy that lies within,

There are no age lines in their faces
Because they partake in nature's graces,
For their happiness abounds in open disguises,
The happy people rejoice at simple themes,
There's no need to make a careful screen:

A bird on the limb of a strong oak tree
Is reason enough to smile at a creature free,
A little green frog in an early spring pond
Is reason enough to cheer it for the run.

A bushy tail squirrel that gives poses in the park
Is reason enough to ignite a happy spark,
A little gray rabbit hopping along a woodland trail
Is reason enough to trigger the happy bell.

The sun that brings forth a bright sunny day
Is reason enough to spark the children to play,
The heavy rain that falls from above
Is reason enough to cultivate the farmer's love.

The roses blossoming in early June
Is reason enough to smile as you work and prune,
To hear the mockingbirds sing and to see the robins fly
Is reason enough to grace the heavens above the sky.
And so you see, there are many reasons to smile
Just observing nature in our little while
On earth to see, to touch, to think, to hear, to smell,
We can experience more of the universe, than we could ever tell!

The Happy People

1. This poem expresses imagery and feelings. Use your imagination! List five examples and tell how each would be active in this poem.
2. Does the poet think that money is a necessity to be happy? Explain your response.
3. How would you describe the mannerisms of a happy person?
4. How does the environment play an important role in the life of a happy person?
5. Does happiness affect the health of a person? Explain.
6. Many health practitioners express the value of laughing or having a smile a day. Would the poet agree with these practitioners? Explain your response.
7. Describe some activities you enjoy in the natural environment.
8. What is your favorite hobby? What do you do in your leisure time?
9. Have you ever spent a day in nature? Write two sentences to describe this experience.
10. Name three things that make you happy. Have you ever done anything to make others happy? Write a short poem about happiness or what makes you happy. You may create your own title.

Dorothy R. Swygert

The Complex Man

"He's complex," so says many,
You're likely to assume that he has plenty
Of time, conversation, love and philosophy
And in his classroom, expertly explains the anatomy
But there's another side to this complex man,
He has not always had the upper hand.

Through hard work and experience, he learned to prod his way.
Many times there were doubts and he bent beneath the sway,
But not once did he concede to find an easy way out,
He held steadfastly to his goal, eventually, winning the bout.

His walk, he treads alone,
Oftentimes, his best friends were gone
In their own direction
Jeering at his predilection
Sneering behind his back
Putting stones on his track
Hoping that he'd fall
And not make it at all
But steadfastly he held on
With the assurance that he was not alone
And straight forward he prevailed
On his future he excelled
And finally, the day shone in bright sunlight,
He was victorious, in pursuing right?

And now, they smile and shake his hand,
Often still trying to decipher, **the complex man!**

Character Building in Youth: The Poetry Workshop

The Complex Man

1. Write a definition for "complex."
2. According to the poet, how many sides are there to this complex man?
3. What is the first impression that one may get from this complex man? Is it good to judge someone by outward appearance without considering the whole person?
4. Describe the complex man in the early years of his life.
5. What is the value of perseverance, that is, not giving up in life?
6. According to the poet, there were many obstacles in the complex man's life. Identify some of these obstacles and explain how he became victorious.
7. Did the complex man have a variety of friends when he was striving to reach his goals?
8. Explain how the complex man remained focused on his goals. Do you have long range and short range goals you are seeking to achieve? Explain.
9. The poet describes the complex man as being successful, "And finally, the day shone in bright sunlight, He was victorious in pursuing right." Write one paragraph explaining this message.
10. What did you like most about his poem? What would you change?
11. Bonus: Do you know a complex man in your family or community? Describe this success story in your own words.

Dorothy R. Swygert

Happiness

Happiness is anything you want it to be
As long as you know from deep within it is true,
Some motives may not be your own,
Especially, when you find, you're beating
Upon a stone,

It's that inner being inside
That will give you the drive
To survive within your stride
And find happiness flourishing right at your side.

Happiness

1. According to the poet, what must one always be if one would like to be happy?
2. What are motives?
3. How may positive motives help one to achieve goals?
4. In line four, what does "beating upon a stone" mean in reference to how one may accomplish his or her dreams"?
5. Where does one get the drive to achieve goals?
6. Explain the meaning in line 7, "To survive within your stride"?
7. Is happiness sometimes misunderstood? Explain.
8. What did you like about this poem?
9. What would you add or change?
10. What things make you happy?

Dorothy R. Swygert

The Nuclear Teen

There is a mother in distress
About her son's educational progress,
She looks up at a kid of 14, standing 6 feet tall
And wonders what decay led to his downfall.

A piercing eye into the past brings many things to light,
A young jolly fellow who was once so, intellectually, bright,
It's hard for a woman to understand
How changes often alters future plans,
Through pre-school, kindergarten, and junior high
What prevented this bird from being able to fly?

Somehow there was a change in commands,
Friends and peers headed for cheers
With little thought of planning for future years,
The bad rags, the smoke bags, the sneakers, and the electronic beepers,
All quiescently saying: "forget the family keepers, "
They are not smart, they are of yesterday's set,
We are in our time and we must not simply be family pets.

We have our own mind to do as we choose
Enjoying life, the sooner the better,
Having fun in ourselves and out-of-ourselves not like a debtor,
We believe in ourselves—we believe in what we do,
It does not matter if what we do is untrue.

The Nuclear Teen

1. What is distress?
2. Identify the characters in this poem.
3. Describe the young man in this poem? What are his mental and physical abilities?
4. Describe the young man's early personality?
5. Why is the young man's mother in distress?
6. Is this family average, poor or well-to-do? Explain.
7. Who were the young man's role models/mentors?
8. Did his mother approve of his role models? Why or why not?
9. Describe the young man's philosophy of life.
10. Explain the last line of this poem, "We believe in ourselves—we believe in what we do, It does not matter if what we do is untrue".
11. Bonus: Recall an article from a local newspaper to describe a person like the poet described in The Nuclear Teen.

Dorothy R. Swygert

The Littlest Babe

There is a little one holding a babe,
An infinite package to serenade,

In young arms, one wonders why
A new life has come down from on high

>Without a marital bond
>A family with deep concern

On how an extended family will survive
Through troubles, hardships, and where poverty thrives.

>A moment of pleasure,
>An earthly defeat,
>An educational life
>that is incomplete.

Who shelters the talent of this little one
That was conceived by teenagers out having fun?

Will it thrive amidst dismal hope and despair,
Grow up to become a tree with rare fruit to bear
Or shiver from the cold of a winter withered tree
Un-nurtured by life and time which must, eventually
>return to Thee?

Character Building in Youth: The Poetry Workshop

The Littlest Babe

Directions: Read the poem to answer the statements below. Write the letter of your choice in the blank provided.

1. ___ The writer has inferred that the mother is:
   a) an adult   b) a teenager   c) middle age
2. ___ The mother of the baby is:
   a) married   b) divorced   c) single
3. ___ The economic life style of the family is:
   a) rich   b) average   c) poor
4. ___ According to the poet, the baby:
   a) was planned b) was unplanned c) was adopted
5. ___ The talents of this baby will probably:
   a) be limited   b) thrive   c) be carefully nurtured
6. ___ According to this writer, having a baby is:
   a) a serious responsibility   b) a fun process   c) an easy task
7. ___ If the baby is successful, the writer compares it to:
   a) a broken arrow   b) a tree with rare fruits   c) a wounded knee
8. ___ If the baby is unsuccessful, the writer compares it to:
   a) a broken arrow   b) a winter withered tree   c) a wounded knee
9. ___ According to the writer, children should be conceived:
   a) in marriage   b) by unmarried teens   c) out of wedlock
10. What would you add to or change about this poem?

Dorothy R. Swygert

The Loafer Shoe

A pair of loafers—good strolling shoes,
The kind of walkers that captures the News:

>The Atlanta Constitution says,
>A shoe that's fit to wear,

>The Birmingham News says,
>They have the Oldie's snare!

>The New York Times sent them to
>Broadway, on loan to "Grease",

>The Village Voice says, they're
>The hottest things to lease,

>The New York Amsterdam hails the
>Shoe in honor of "tapping" Bill,

>The Chicago Defender advertises them
>For a night and a thrill,

>The San Francisco Times displays them
>For dancing to the rhymes,

>The children of Harlem says, for any time,

A slot for pennies, a smart grain of leather,
A pair of shoes, for any kind of weather,
Snugly fit on happy feet,
So don't be slow, don't miss the beat.
Give yourself, the LOAFER treat!

Character Building in Youth: The Poetry Workshop

The Loafer Shoe

Directions: Read "The Loafer Shoe" carefully to complete the exercise below. Match each state with the correct newspaper. Write the letter of your choice in the blank provided.

State   Newspaper
___1. New York   A. Chicago Defender
___2. Georgia   B. San Francisco Times
___3. California   C. Village Voice
___4. Alabama   D. Atlanta Constitution
___5. Illinois   E. Birmingham News

Directions: Read the poem, The *Loafer Shoe,* carefully to complete this exercise. Match Column A with Column B by matching the activity with the correct newspaper. Write the letter of your choice in the blank provided.

Column A   Column B
____1. "dancing to the rhymes"   A. Chicago Defender
____2. "shoe that's fit to wear"   B. San Francisco Times
____3. "hottest things to lease"   C. Village Voice
____4. "a night and a thrill"   D. Birmingham News
____5. "on Broadway on loan to Grease" E. Atlanta Constitution
____6. "in honor of tapping Bill"   F. New York Amsterdam
____7. "they have the oldest snare"   G. New York Times

Dorothy R. Swygert

Directions: You have been selected to give an audition for a performance of the poem, *The Loafer Shoe*. You are to select a group to present this performance to the buyers of Macy's Department Store. You are responsible for creating this skit and designing your wardrobe centered around the loafer shoe. Macy's is going to introduce a new line in the fall to showcase this product. You are to create your clothing for each activity theme in the poem to depict and highlight each newspaper and coordinate each pair of loafers with the wardrobes you have designed. You will be responsible for the music and the choreography of this showcase performance. If you are successful, you will be given a contract with this department store. Summarize this request in writing to share with the buyers one month in advance.

Character Building in Youth: The Poetry Workshop

Dorothy R. Swygert

THE OEPHOEBIC OATH
(School Graduation)

We, the Graduating Class of __, realize that we
have not come to this point of life alone.
As we look back at our steps in life we see parents,
friends, kin, neighbors, principals,
teachers, counselors and deans who have played an
important role in helping us through our school years.

In a time where there is a great need for positive changes
in every avenue of our society,
We, the Graduating Class of __, pledge to hold our
heads high as we strive to
(develop our talents) mold and shape a new generation
through love, honesty and pride.

We further pledge to respect one another and to
Recognize the high quality of life.
We look up to the Guiding Light of Life to strengthen
Us and to give us a sense of direction
That we may achieve
A better way of life

OEPHOEBIC OATH
(School Graduation)

1. Is this a happy day for the graduate? Why? Explain your answer in one sentence.
2. Have you ever attended a graduation? Describe the joy of such an occasion.
3. Graduation is a milestone in the life of a person. Did the graduate accomplish this achievement alone? Explain.
4. According to the author, what contributions to society can be made by graduates?
5. What three virtues are the graduates challenged to use in molding and shaping a new generation?
6. What two pledges do the graduates make to one another?
7. Name some people in the community who supported the graduate in realizing this goal.
8. What personnel from the school played an important role in assisting the graduate to reach this milestone in life?
9. How can these graduates continue to develop their gifts and talents?
10. What can these graduates do to continue to building a better way of life?

Dorothy R. Swygert

A Pledge of a Full-Fledged Human Being
(Being the Best I Can Be)

I, PLEDGE to direct my attention to developing my abilities and talents by striving to do my best work in school, attending and arriving to all classes on time.

I will not be satisfied with a grade of 65 when I can do better. I will raise my LEVEL OF CONSCIOUSNESS to recognize and respect the QUALITY OF LIFE. I will remind myself every day that **I AM SOMEBODY** and that I have a positive contribution to make in this life by helping myself and others.

I will engage my mind and my leisure time in positive activities. I will spend my leisure time nurturing and developing my talents so that I may BECOME THE BEST PERSON I am capable of becoming.

Yes, I will remember I am a role model for my younger brothers and sisters, friends and kin, therefore, I will be conscious of BEING THE BEST I CAN BE so I can, BEGINNING TODAY, in this world, MAKE A BETTER TOMORROW.

A Pledge of a Full Fledged Human Being
(Being the Best I Can Be)

Directions: Read this pledge carefully to engage in the exercise below. The title for this work is *My Philosophy of Life*. You are to select eight goals from this poem to list as your philosophy. The first one has been written for you. After reading the poem carefully, you will write the remaining seven goals as a background for writing a brief essay describing your philosophy of life.

1. I will set aside time to develop my gifts and talents.
2.
3.
4.
5.
6.
7.
8.

Write a one page essay describing your Philosophy of Life.

Dorothy R. Swygert

From Your Daughter, Dad, On Father's Day

Dad, I am not your little girl anymore
But, you would be proud of the woman you have
cultivated:

From your living model, I learned the charm
of family life and motherhood,
The joy of living and doing good,
Teaching, loving and being understood,
For it was under your guidance that the light began
to shine
With virtue and truth from life's nurturing vine.

You planted the seed where the bud bloomed
And now, as I plant my garden, I will remember to
Nurture the seed on air, sunshine and rain,
The gifts of God in a sweet refrain
And so you see, nurturing a good seed will never
cease,
It simply, unfolds in God's inner peace.

HAPPY FATHER'S DAY!

From Your Daughter, Dad, On Father's Day

1. What stage of growth is this female?
2. What does it mean to reminisce?
3. Why has this female taken out time to reminisce?
4. According to the writer, did this female enjoy a beautiful childhood? Explain.
5. What is the special occasion?
6. Give an interpretation of the line, "life's nurturing vine."
7. Write an interpretation for the metaphor "And now, as I plant my garden."
8. Who was the living model for this female? Explain.
9. What synonym would you use for *seed* in this poem?
10. Write a sentence explaining the line, "The joy of living and doing good."

Dorothy R. Swygert

MOTHERS ARE SPECIAL

Mothers are special, it's plain to see
That they spring forth from nature's tree,
With hands that create activities for work and play
And a kind smile that washes the tears away,
A warm heart that is quick to understand,
The gentle voice that teaches without command,
She works off-schedule around the clock
And is never too busy to help the kid around the block,
Her love is plentiful and spreads to all,
She is never too busy to answer a neighbor's call,
When God, above, created mother
He daunted her with love, like none other

HAPPY MOTHER'S DAY!

MOTHERS ARE SPECIAL

1. What line(s) of this poem defines mothers as being special?
2. What is the value of a smile in this poem? How does a smile make you feel when you are sad?
3. What difference does a warm smile makes when you are trying to explain a difficult situation?
4. Some people believe a soft voice can teach without command. Do you agree or disagree?
5. According to this poem, "A mother's day is never done." Write an interpretation for this line.
6. What does the poet implies when she says, "Her love is plentiful and spreads to all?"
7. Is the mother described as a good neighbor in this poem? Identify the line that supports your response?
8. Mother, in this poem, is described in figurative language as "falling from nature's tree." Write a synonym for nature's tree.
9. The traditional working hours for an employee have been defined by Dolly Parton's song as *9 to 5*. Can you count the working hours for the mother as described in this poem?
10. Write a short poem to describe your mother.

Dorothy R. Swygert

Family Heritage on Father's Day

When I think of you Dad, I think of the warm chats
We shared around the fireplace,
The strength and love of those gatherings
helped to mold and shape my views
on family life.

As I keep passing the torch of family life,
My heart swells with pride with the memories
And values I cherish from my past.
And now, as I look back and press forward
I can pass the Torch and tell the next generation to:
Keep the home fires burning.

Happy Father's Day!

Define the Role of a Father in Our Times

Write a one-page composition to define [what you think is] the role of a father.

Dorothy R. Swygert

Spread Your Wings

For the Lord gives wisdom:
Out of his mouth comes knowledge
and understanding. Proverb 2:6.

Spread your wings, old great eagle,
Spread them wide and far,
For it is only when you stretch yourself
That you may reach your star:

With wisdom, you've ripened with age,
With time, you've learned to use it wisely,
With patience, you've learned to cultivate
      it in life's tasks,
With discipline, you've learned to hold
      your temper and tongue,
With persistence, you've worked to develop
      your mind,
With knowledge, you've increased your
      understanding,
With understanding, you've graced the
minds of the young,

Endurance has been a long and painstakingly task
      but you've learned it well,
Of life's difficult lessons to tell
Through knowledge and wisdom you've excelled
So you have earned the right to stretch your wings,
Stretch them wide and far
For you have overcome life's obstacles and you have
      earned your STAR!

Spread Your Wings

1. Write a poem about a person in your community, church or school whose life is a model of *Spread Your Wings*.

Dorothy R. Swygert

DARE TO BE DIFFERENT

There is more to life than exploiting your body
    by becoming a premature mother, an unequipped father.
There is more to life than being
    an inmate behind a prison wall
Where the dew drops of life never
    rises to embrace that
    magnificent person God
    meant you to be.

There is more to life than having the sharpest tongue
rolling vulgar and profane language off your lips
that God made to be a great orator, singer or speaker.

There is more to life than being a conformist
ridiculing the "nerd" or
the "goody-goody" child,

Dare to be different—to be

great in unison—in oneness

    with God,
    ....**Our Creator.**

DARE TO BE DIFFERENT!

Directions: Write three paragraphs expressing what *"Dare to be Different"* means to you as you pursue your journey in life.

Addendum:

PERSONAL GROWTH

AND

DEVELOPMENT

My Career Preparation

- My Career Interest
- My Talents, Skills and Gifts
- How do my talents complement my career interest?

Reading Books and Biographies:

Title	Author	Date Completed
_____	_____	_____
_____	_____	_____
_____	_____	_____
_____	_____	_____
_____		

- My Career Research

Setting Goals and Reaching High

- Write a definition for goal:
- Describe what it means to take the necessary steps to reach a goal:
- My short-range goals: (what you are planning to do within a time period of one year)
- Steps I will take to achieve my short-range goals:
- My long range-goals: (what you are planning to do within three to five years)
- Steps I will take to achieve my long-range goals:

Dorothy R. Swygert

My Biography
(Brainstorming)

- Family Information:
    - Family Background:
    - Parents' Careers:
- Civic and Community Work and Participation:
- Summarize your talents:
- Summarize how you use the above:
- My goal:
- My interests:
- My aspirations:
- Who are your models/mentors? (Individual who has been a positive influence in your life)
- My Career Interest:
- Describe what makes you happy in life.
- How do you cope with disappointment?
- List your honors, awards and honorable mentions.
- Are you an honor roll student?
- What are your hobbies?
- What do you do in your leisure time?
- Describe your best vacation

My Philosophy of Life

- Write a definition for philosophy of life:
- Describe your personality: (Are you a leader or a follower?)
- Do you have a set of rules [inside you] to guide you on life's journey?
- Describe your value system:
- Do you know when to be with the crowd and when to be an individual? Explain.
- How do you plan to use your gifts and talents in life?
- **What is most important to you? Being able to make the largest salary to enhance your profile or to make a decent salary and be able to give back to uplift humanity?**
- Have you identified your purpose in life? What steps will you take to make this a reality?
- Are you a positive role model or mentor for your younger siblings and other youth in your community? Give two examples.

Dorothy R. Swygert

Worthy Home Membership: Family Devotion

- What are your tasks and responsibilities in your home?
- Do you take pride in building your community? How do you contribute to making a positive difference on your block?
- Do you plan your wardrobe and make preparation for the next day? What do you do the night before?
- How is your time management? Describe how you use your time to be successful.
- How do you share with the family? Do you engage in a family hour, dinner hour?
- Do you share your talents and achievements with your family?
- Do you set aside a quiet time on a daily basis for your self?
- Do you maintain a journal of daily events?
- Do you read the Bible, poetry and other literature?
- What is the name of the best book you have read?

Volunteer Services: Resume Builder

- Do you participate in community service? Explain:
- What extra-curricular activities are you affiliated with in church, school and community?
- Do you engage in part-time work? Explain:

Reading Habits:

- How many books do you read each month? Give title and author of two books.
- Do you read the newspaper and other periodicals on a daily basis? List three newspapers.

Money and the Use of Money:

- Do you have a savings account or plan? Have you disciplined yourself in financial affairs? Are you in debt? Why? What are your plans to close this debt account? Do you know your credit rating?

Dorothy R. Swygert

Individual Assessment: My Gifts and Talents

- List your gifts and talents (my strengths):
- What skills do you have? (typing, computer, technology, graphics, repair bikes, etc)
- How can these talents and skills help you in starting your own business?
- List three things you do not do well, that are needed in your business:
- What is your career interest? What would you like to become?

A Community Analysis

Do a survey of your community. Look around in your community to answer the questions below.

- Describe your community:
- What do you like about your community?
- What do you dislike about your community?
- What would you like to change about your community?
- What services or businesses would you like to have in your community? How would these services make a positive difference in your community?

Dorothy R. Swygert

Building Community Today for Tomorrow

- Identify and list some of your gifts, skills and talents:
- How do you plan to use these gifts, skills and talents in your life?
- How are you preparing yourself today to actualize these gifts, skills and talents? In 1947, Dr. Martin L. King, Jr. wrote an essay in college, *The Purpose of Education*. This essay was published in the *Maroon Tiger* at Morehouse. He defined education as having two components, intelligence and character.
- **Define and contrast the meaning of intelligence and character.**
- Do you have a desire to start your own business? If you could, what business would you develop? Why? Would this business contribute to the building of a positive community? Explain.
- Identify some things you would need to do in order to maintain your business. What contribution would you make to the community?

Character Building in Youth: The Poetry Workshop

COURTESY
&
RECONCILIATION

What ever happened to the social amenities of life?

A Request: "Please"

A Favor: "Thank you"

A Mistake: "Excuse Me"

An Error: "I'm Sorry"

A Bad Deed: "Please Forgive Me!"

To Share: "Would You Like …"

A Kind Deed: "A Note Expressing Thanks"

Rekindle The ♥

Dorothy R. Swygert

I Am Somebody
Cultivating My Life With Hope

To all people out in the world, I have a message for you. Here is a world report from me to you. I would like people to know I am an upbeat person. I have a positive personality. I do not believe anyone can keep me down if I want to be up. To all you readers out there, I want you to know I am a person of quality. If you do not understand my language, keep your eyes on this page and you will understand. You see, I look into the mirror everyday and compliment myself. Do not get me wrong, that is not being narcissistic or being hung up on myself, it is just normal behavior. *Think about it! If you plan to succeed in this life on this planet, you must feel good about yourself.* Do not take away from the Creator. Give thanks for your blessing of life. Remember, you must do your part in strengthening your heart to realize the greatness of your being.

The first thing you need to do is to give yourself a good start by kissing the dawning of the day. To make this day complete, there are three things you must know about yourself. *Firstly, you must know that you are somebody going somewhere in life to make a positive difference.* And if you know that you are somebody, then act and carry yourself as if you are somebody. When you hold yourself in high regards, then you do not embarrass your Creator by going into the world looking at other human copies and wishing you looked like them. You look into your mirror and appreciate what you see, smile with thanksgiving for what you see and give appreciation for the gifts you have been given to travel this human pathway.

Secondly, you must know that you are going somewhere in life because you have been blessed with some gifts, skills and talents. You may not have the same talents as others whom you meet along your journey, but you do have your gift package, that when properly used, will provide you with the means to not only survive but to help others in life. Help may be seen in different ways, not necessarily from the hip, but from your lips or with other gifts. You may be a creative artist or an inventor. *Whatever your talents, your responsibility is to identify and develop them in a positive way to help yourself and others.*

Thirdly, the goal that you are going somewhere in life to make a positive difference must be made a reality as you make this journey along the human pathway. *You do not know how much time the Creator has allotted you. Consequently, you must view your journey with a serious heart in using each day to the fullest in realizing your talents.* You do not have time to be a procrastinator, always putting things off for tomorrow. You must perceive everyday as an opportunity to promote your human package and share the wealth. You must count each day as a blessing. When you look at others, wear a smile on your face and utter words of encouragement.

As you give to others, you must not lose sight of your own goals and the steps and stages you must pursue in order to fulfill them. You must respect the differences of others with hope that others, too, will respect you. But if they do not, you still have the responsibility to fulfill the purpose the Creator has entrusted to you. By doing this, you can become the greatest person you are capable of being, as well as to make a positive difference in building a better world. Remember, you must stay focused on the prize!

Dorothy R. Swygert

Take Away Package

Questions

1. How would you describe the person in this article? What does it means to be an upbeat person?
2. According to the writer, what is the first thing one should do in the morning? Why does the writer think this act is important?
3. Describe three things the writer says everyone should do.
4. What is the meaning of narcissism?
5. Describe the "human package" that one receives for his/her journey in life.
6. Have you ever wished that you were someone else or looked like someone else? Give an example.
7. Describe your human package. How are you using this package?
8. How does the writer feel about procrastination? Is this a good character trait?
9. According to the writer, the Creator plays an important role in preparing one for life's journey. Explain. Give examples.
10. How can human beings help each other to succeed in life? What is camaraderie?

MY POETRY

Dorothy R. Swygert

MY POETRY

MY POETRY

Dorothy R. Swygert

MY POETRY

MY POETRY

Dorothy R. Swygert

MY POETRY

MY POETRY

Dorothy R. Swygert

MY POETRY

MY POETRY

Dorothy R. Swygert

MY POETRY

MY POETRY

Dorothy R. Swygert

MY POETRY

Character Building in Youth: The Poetry Workshop

MY POETRY

Dorothy R. Swygert

MY POETRY

MY POETRY

Dorothy R. Swygert

MY POETRY

MY POETRY

Dorothy R. Swygert

MY POETRY

MY POETRY

Dorothy R. Swygert

MY POETRY

MY POETRY

Dorothy R. Swygert

MY POETRY

Dr. Dorothy R. Swygert

The Heart of this Woman

Philosophy of Life

Each individual is born into this world with gifts and talents. The goal for each should be to develop these gifts and talents and use them in a positive way to help themselves and others, to help make this a better world.

Philosophy of Education

Dorothy Swygert has an abiding faith in making the best education available to all children. In summarizing her philosophy of education, she says, "All children can learn. They may not learn in the same modality, but all children can learn. Children are very perceptive. They know when you love them and when you do not." She believes that educational services should be provided to nurture the gifts and talents for all children, thus providing for a more just society.

Hope

What is hope to Dorothy Swygert? The joy of loving children is to see hope sparkle in their eyes. She says, "The child is like a tender plant. If you water and nurture the plant, it will grow and blossom in beauty with its natural juices spraying a mist of sweet fragrances. If we service and nurture our children, they will grow to build a just nation."

Parent

Dorothy Swygert was married to Mack D. Swygert, Jr. until his death, and from this union, they were blessed with two sons. Her oldest son is a graduate of Alabama A & M University and the youngest earned graduate degrees from Hampton and Howard Universities.

Education
Dorothy R. Swygert earned graduate degrees in guidance, supervision and administration from New York University.

Dorothy R. Swygert

Dr. Swygert's Lantern to Parents and Guardians

The educational process begins in the home, the primary agent of children. Parents and guardians can play a vital role in preparing children to obtain quality education. To make this as brief as possible, I will list ten things you may do to begin fulfilling your role and handling your responsibility.

1. Create a warm loving *learning environment for your child*. Let your child know that education is very important. Teach your child to love and appreciate books at an early age. Set aside time each night to read a story to the pre-K to third grader before retiring. Laugh, smile, joke and have fun as you read the story. Make bedtime a fun time. Create a neat book corner to remove and replace books. When the books are removed, the child has the responsibility of returning them to the proper place.
2. Teach your child the *social amenities of life*. Bond your child to embrace your morals and standards. Teach your child to be kind, courteous and polite in social situations. Teach your child to respect the rights of others.
3. Assign *age-level tasks* to your child. For example, he or she can put away the lunch box, be responsible for securing his/her belongings (hat, coat, gloves, scarf, etc.), bring school assignments home (homework) and share the school day with you. Always remember to thank the child for remembering to bring school assignments home and for sharing them with you. This behavior will reinforce a good habit.
4. Use the internet or yellow pages *to locate teachers' stores* and others that sell educational supplies (math flash cards, sight words,

phonics sets, time tables, geometrical designs, etc.). Invest in educational aids to enhance your child's growth and development. Include these educational tools in your budget to prepare your child to develop his/her skills, talents and abilities.

5. Teach your child to take pride in doing the best work possible. Create little rewards and incentives to encourage top-level performance in school.
6. Guide your child in *learning gracious social skills*. The child should learn to respect the rights of others. The child should learn how to socialize with his/her age level, but should know the time to be an individual and when to be with the group. Teach your child how to discern right from wrong. Example: It is wrong to take another person's belongings without permission; it is wrong to instigate fights.
7. Teach your child to *respect humanity*, that is, that every person is important. Be kind and respectful to all people.
8. Teach your child how to follow-up on disagreements using the proper ladder of referral (teacher, dean, principal, etc.).
9. Create a folder for each child in your household. This file will hold pertinent information on each child (grade, teacher, school address, daily schedule and teachers, health record, report card, etc.).
10. Keep a school calendar of dates and events for the school year. Remember you, as the parent/guardian, are important in the home-school community network. Place the important dates on your personal calendar. Attend PTA, local school board and other meetings pertaining to your child's educational progress. Your presence will insure that you will participate in the policy making and decision making process in your quest to achieve quality education for your child and the children in your community. Block by block, as you communicate with other parents/guardians, you will be able to make a difference.